CONTENTS

CHAPTER ONE

MOON MISSIONS PAST AND PRESENT

Imagine you live in space. You're **orbiting** the Moon aboard a new space station. The air smells of a weird mix of rubbish and cleaning supplies. Fans and pumps hum as they constantly work to keep the air around you clean. LED lights make it feel like daytime. Through the window, you can see clouds swirling over the blue globe of Earth.

Your day begins in the laboratory, doing science experiments. Later, your spacecraft travels closer to the Moon. You can see its craters and peaks clearly. Conditions are great for a trip to the surface. Dressed in your spacesuit, you collect rock and dust samples to bring back to the station. You hope to learn more about the history of the Moon and Earth from these samples.

MOON BASE AND BEYOND

THE LUNAR GATEWAY TO DEEP SPACE

ALICIA Z. KLEPEIS

Raintree is an imprint of Capstone Global Library Limited, a company incorporated in England and Wales having its registered office at 264 Banbury Road, Oxford, OX2 7DY – Registered company number: 6695582

www.raintree.co.uk
myorders@raintree.co.uk

Editor: Mandy Robbins
Designer: Laura Mitchell
Media researcher: Jo Miller
Original illustrations © Capstone Global Library Limited 2020
Production Specialist: Katy LaVigne
Originated by Capstone Global Library Ltd
Printed and bound in India

ISBN 978 1 4747 8839 7 (hardback)
ISBN 978 1 4747 8849 6 (paperback)

British Library Cataloguing in Publication Data
A full catalogue record for this book is available from the British Library.

Acknowledgements
We would like to thank Sarah Ruiz, an aerospace engineer with NASA, for her invaluable help in the preparation of this book. We would like to thank the following for permission to reproduce photographs: NASA, Cover (spacecraft), 1 (spacecraft), 7, 9, 11, 13, 15, 16–17, 19, 21, 26; Science Source: Chris Butler, 23, ESA/Foster + Partners, 25, Victor Habbick Visions, 29; Shutterstock: Belish, Cover (Moon), 1 (Moon), Romolo Tavani, 5
Design Elements: Capstone; Shutterstock: Audrius Birbilas.

Imagine living on the Moon and seeing Earth in the sky, just as you see the Moon now.

This scenario might seem far off in the future. But it's not. Astronauts could be living and researching in **lunar** orbit and on the surface of the Moon by the mid-2020s.

SPACE FACT

We always see the same side of the Moon from Earth. That's because it spins around at the same rate that it orbits Earth.

lunar having to do with a moon

orbit to travel around an object in space; an orbit is also the path an object follows while circling an object in space

EARLY MOON EXPLORATION

The Moon has fascinated people for thousands of years. But humans didn't have the technology to get there until the 1950s. In 1959, the former Soviet Union successfully landed a small spacecraft called Luna 2 on the Moon. Between 1968 and 1972, the United States' National Aeronautics and Space Administration (NASA) sent nine manned missions to the Moon. Japan, China and India have sent unmanned missions to the Moon too.

Today the United States has a new plan called Space Policy Directive 1. It puts exploring the Moon at the top of NASA's "to-do" list for the first time in nearly 50 years. But the way astronauts explore the Moon will change. The Apollo 11 crew that landed on the Moon in 1969 spent less than 22 hours there. Future astronauts might spend six weeks at a time circling the Moon and exploring its surface. Eventually, the Moon could be a jumping off point for places further out in deep space, to Mars and beyond!

SPACE FACT

Technology has come a long way since the first Moon missions. A smartphone has more computing power than NASA had during the 1960s and early 1970s.

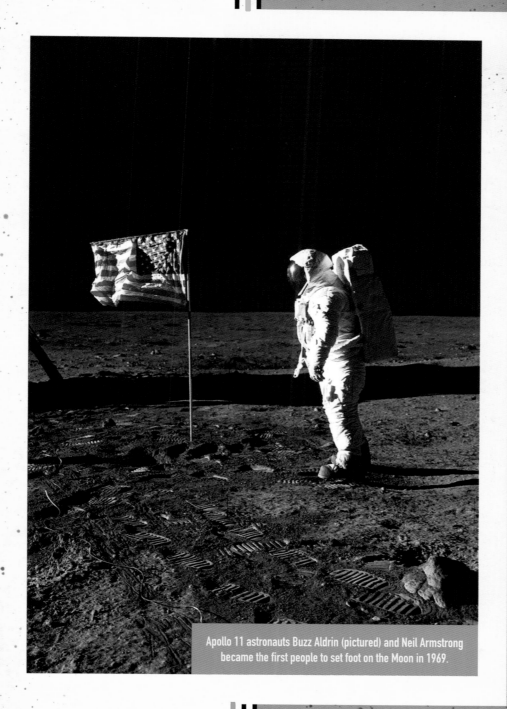

Apollo 11 astronauts Buzz Aldrin (pictured) and Neil Armstrong became the first people to set foot on the Moon in 1969.

CHAPTER TWO

GATEWAY

NASA is leading an international effort to
build the Lunar Orbital Platform-Gateway.
This mini space station, nicknamed "Gateway",
will orbit the Moon. Astronaut crews will live and
work there. They will test new technologies for
exploring in deep space. Crews will stay at the
Gateway for up to six weeks. Even when no one
is living there, scientific
tools on the inside
and outside of
Gateway will
continue to
gather data.

SPACE FACT

The European, Japanese and
Canadian space agencies plan to
use Gateway for a robotic mission
to the Moon in the 2020s.

Designers have gone through several versions of what Gateway's design will be.

Astronauts at Gateway will also make judgements about possible living arrangements for future missions. Perhaps they will discover that such a small space is not suitable for long-term missions. They might find better ways to arrange and use the small spaces they have. Astronauts living on the International Space Station (ISS) today have much more space than those on Gateway will. The inside of the ISS is about the size of a five-bedroom house. But Gateway will be more like living in a camper van.

	GATEWAY	ISS
WEIGHT	68 TONNES	408 TONNES
DISTANCE FROM EARTH	MORE THAN 200,000 MILES (322,000 KM)	250 MILES (402 KM)
HABITABLE MODULES*	2–3	15
NUMBER OF RESIDENTS	4	6
LENGTH OF STAY	UP TO 6 WEEKS	UP TO 6 MONTHS (TYPICALLY)

POWER AND · · · ·
PROPULSION UNIT

GATEWAY'S DESIGN

Engineers have designed Gateway to have six or seven units called **modules**. They will fit together to form the station. Each module will have a specific purpose. There will probably be two modules to house the astronauts. The astronauts will live and do research there. Another module will provide solar electric power. That electricity will power the station's lights, computers, fans and more.

ROBOTIC ARM

ORION SPACECRAFT

PROPELLANT STORAGE, AND TELECOMMUNICATIONS

CARGO DELIVERY MODULE

E

A   B   C   D   F   G   H   I

ROBOTIC VEHICLE FOR LUNAR MISSIONS

AIRLOCK

POSSIBLE ADDITIONAL HOUSING AND WORK SPACE

ASTRONAUT HOUSING AND WORK SPACE

ASTRONAUT HOUSING AND WORK SPACE

One module will serve as a docking port. This is a bit like a garage, where spacecraft coming to Gateway can both "park" and depart from. It will also serve as an **airlock** for astronauts going on **spacewalks**. There will also be modules for power storage and communication, as well as for intake of **cargo** deliveries. A final module called the Orion Spacecraft could carry the crew out into deep space.

airlock enclosure between two airtight doors to permit passage from one space to the other

cargo goods carried by a vehicle

module separate section that can be linked to other parts

spacewalk period of time during which an astronaut leaves the spacecraft to move around in space

BUILDING GATEWAY

So how and where will Gateway be built? The plan is for unmanned rockets to send the various parts for Gateway into space. The lunar modules will then be assembled while in orbit.

The first Gateway hardware is scheduled to ship from Earth in 2022. The power and **propulsion** element (PPE) will be shipped from Earth first. The PPE will maintain Gateway's position and move it between different locations. The PPE will also provide Gateway's communications. Several other parts will be launched after the PPE, followed by the airlock. Later on, another module will allow cargo missions to take supplies to the Gateway.

How an airlock works

Humans can't breathe in space. Because of this, space stations must have something called an airlock. It is a small room between outer space and the space station. It keeps the air from leaking out of the space station. To go on a spacewalk, an astronaut dressed in a spacesuit would step into the airlock. The outside door would be closed. Once inside, the astronaut would close the inside door. All of the air would then be pumped out of the airlock. Then the astronaut would open the outside door and head into space.

Special ropes called tethers fasten astronauts to the spacecraft so they don't float away.

Building Gateway is likely to be an international effort. Russia may be building the airlock module. Japan may provide a unit to help with communications and propulsion. Canada might construct a robotic arm for outdoor work at Gateway. NASA will provide one housing module. One of its international partners will provide the other. Scientists from around the world could benefit from Gateway. NASA officials think the Gateway could be ready to house astronauts by the mid-2020s.

propulsion thrust or power that makes an aircraft or spacecraft move forward

CHAPTER THREE

MOON VEHICLES AND LANDING

Space agencies and private companies are currently working on developing new space vehicles. One spacecraft is called Orion. Astronauts will travel to and from Gateway in Orion. This exploration vehicle is built for deep space. Orion could travel to Mars or even an asteroid.

Orion needs a boost to be lifted into orbit. So it will launch on top of a giant rocket called the Space Launch System (SLS). It will be able to launch Orion while also carrying heavy cargo, such as Gateway modules and landers. It will carry more cargo to lunar orbit than any previous vehicles.

SPACE FACT

Shipping items from Earth into space can cost more than £19,500 per 0.50 kilogram (1 pound)!

The Launch Abort System (LAS) is an important part of Orion. In case of an emergency during launch, the LAS would propel the crew module a safe distance away from the rocket. A parachute system would allow the module to land safely back on the ground. The LAS breaks away once Orion reaches orbit.

LANDING ON THE MOON

When the Apollo spacecraft travelled to the
Moon, it flew in a circular path about 100 kilometres
(60 miles) from the Moon's surface. It was only able to
land near the Moon's **equator**. That won't be the case
with Gateway.

Gateway's orbit will vary in its distance to the
Moon's surface. The astronauts aboard Gateway
will be able to choose where they want to land on
the Moon's surface. This will give them far more
opportunities to learn about different parts of the
Moon. The parts can include the Moon's poles, impact
craters and **lava tubes**.

Once Gateway crew members choose a location, they will take a special landing vehicle down to the surface. In the past, different rovers or lunar vehicles explored the Moon's surface and were then left behind. They are all still on the Moon! Today space agencies are working to develop reusable vehicles to explore on future missions.

SPACE FACT

Scientists have tested the incredible 3 metre- (10 foot-) tall Lunar Electric Rover in the Arizona desert in the United States. Its pressurized cabin has fold-down beds, a sink, a toilet and a collapsible exercise bike!

equator imaginary line around the middle of a planet or body in space

lava tube a natural tunnel formed by a lava flow

CHAPTER FOUR

SCIENCE IN SPACE

Humans have already been to the Moon. They've collected rocks from its surface. **Probes** have provided scientists with loads of information. But they have only scratched the surface. There's still so much to learn about the Moon and deep space beyond.

Instruments mounted on the outside of Gateway will help make observations of Earth, the Moon and the solar system. Scientists will also operate robots remotely to explore the Moon's surface more closely. Unlike humans, robots could explore in the vacuum of space without time limits. They could also gather samples on the Moon's surface and take them to Gateway for astronauts to study.

The Japanese NanoRacks CubeSat Deployer sends out a set of CubeSats from the ISS in 2014.

Astronauts will send CubeSats from Gateway as well. A CubeSat is a tiny cube-shaped research spacecraft. It's only about 10 centimetres (4 inches) long and weighs 1.4 kilograms (3 pounds). These tiny **satellites** could investigate asteroids or measure **radiation**. They may also seek out future landing sites at different locations in space.

SPACE FACT

Two CubeSats, nicknamed "Wall-E" and "Eva", were the first to travel to another planet. They headed to Mars in May 2018. They completed their mission in November 2018.

probe small vehicle used to explore objects in outer space

radiation dangerous rays of energy given off by certain elements

satellite an object that moves around a cosmic body; a spacecraft used to send signals and information from one place to another

HUMANS IN DEEP SPACE

One goal of going back to the Moon is to learn more about how deep space affects the human body. ISS crew members have made many discoveries through experiments using their own bodies. For example, they have found it is possible to reduce the bone and muscle loss in space with certain exercises.

You may wonder, if astronauts can learn about their bodies in space on the ISS, why travel further from Earth? Deep space may affect the human body in different ways from low-Earth orbit. Scientists need to know more about the risks of radiation exposure in deep space before sending astronauts to Mars and beyond.

Crews aboard the Gateway will also have to hone their survival skills in deep space. They'll have to train for emergency situations in which they would be too far to get help from Earth. Machinery might break. A crew member might have a serious health crisis. Astronauts need to plan how to solve possible problems before they occur millions of kilometres from home.

Astronauts on the ISS exercise about two hours a day to keep muscles and bones from getting weak.

CHAPTER FIVE

A LUNAR COLONY

People have dreamed of living on the Moon for hundreds of years. But there are many challenges to living there. There is no oxygen to breathe. The temperature swings from minus 233 degrees Celsius (minus 387 degrees Fahrenheit) at night to 123°C (253°F) during the day. There is also no **atmosphere** to protect humans from the Sun's dangerous radiation.

SPACE FACT

New research suggests that concrete made of Moon soil and rocks could be stronger than concrete made on Earth.

A Moon habitat would have to be airtight. It would have to provide a steady stream of breathable air for its residents without leaking. It would also need to be temperature controlled. A Moon habitat must be very strong and sturdy. It would have to withstand space rocks that often rain down onto the Moon's surface. It would need a water recycling system. A system to generate power would also be needed. A place would be needed for residents to store and prepare food. It may even have a place for residents to grow food. The technology for such a plan is just starting to be developed.

atmosphere layer of gases that surrounds some planets, dwarf planets and moons

BUILDING A MOON BASE

Building a Moon base would be an enormous undertaking. Some experts think a great location might be in the deep craters near the Moon's poles. These super-cold locations probably contain frozen water. Astronauts could use the water as a resource.

According to NASA, before construction for a Moon base begins, robots might build the landing site for a Moon outpost. Two robots could stabilize the Moon's loose soil. They would also build walls around the launch pads. Using robots would be safer and less expensive than having people do this kind of construction.

Water on the Moon

For many years, people thought the Moon was completely dry. But in 2009, a satellite called the Lunar Crater Observation and Sensing Satellite (LCROSS) proved them wrong. The LCROSS was purposely crashed into a crater near the Moon's south pole. The crash kicked up more than 98 litres (26 gallons) of water! This could provide a vital lifeline to those visiting or living on the Moon.

The European Space Agency is researching the possibility of building a Moon base like the one pictured using lunar soil via a 3-D printer.

What might the construction process look like? First, a space rocket would transport the base of the Moon **colony**. It would be folded up into a tube-shaped module. Next, an inflatable dome would stretch from one end of the module to the other. This would provide a sturdy support structure for construction. Then a robot-operated 3-D printer would make building blocks out of the Moon's own dust, soil and rock. These would go over the dome and provide a protective shell for the lunar base.

colony place where a group of people have gone to live with the intention of staying

Astronaut Don Petit floats among several bags of rubbish before they are thrown out of the ISS.

To PMA2 DECK

SPACE FACT

Past lunar missions have left some interesting waste on the Moon. It includes three lunar rovers, several cameras, a family photo and nearly 100 bags of human waste.

HUMANS IN DEEP SPACE

Whether on Earth or in space, people must eat and throw away their rubbish. But these tasks are more difficult and expensive in deep space. Humans must find creative options. NASA scientists think it may be possible for astronauts to grow plants while living on the Moon.

In the future, "space farms" may provide much of the food needed by astronauts. These indoor greenhouses will have special lamps to help plants thrive in the controlled environment of a spacecraft. Space gardens could also recycle waste and make more oxygen. For long trips into space, freshly grown produce would have more nutrients than food brought from Earth months earlier.

Managing rubbish in deep space will be a real challenge. ISS rubbish is loaded onto empty cargo ships and burned up during the trip back down through Earth's atmosphere. But there won't be as many resupply missions to Gateway as there are to the ISS. Companies are developing ways of squeezing rubbish to make it easier to store. NASA is also exploring the use of **biodegradable** packaging material.

biodegradable substance or object that breaks down naturally in the environment

THE FUTURE OF
SPACE EXPLORATION

Over the next 10 years, astronauts will probably learn a great deal about living and researching in deep space from the area near the Moon. But in the near future, Gateway may serve as a jumping off point for missions to Mars and beyond.

It's an exciting time for space exploration and scientific discoveries. We could discover more about the human body in deep space, about the Moon and about what lies beyond. But it will take an international effort to tackle the challenges of being further away from the comforts of Earth.

Maybe you will be an astronaut or a space tourist in the future. You might drop off supplies at Gateway for crew members on their way to an asteroid. Or maybe you'll build a space farm that will feed the hungry residents of a Moon colony. In the not-too-distant future, maybe you'll help mine asteroids or leave your boot prints on Mars' red soil!

It may not be long before humans have a thriving colony on the Moon!

GLOSSARY

airlock enclosure between two airtight doors to allow passage from one space to the other

atmosphere layer of gases that surrounds some planets, dwarf planets and moons

biodegradable substance or object that breaks down naturally in the environment

cargo goods transported in a vehicle, ship or aircraft

colony place where a group of people have gone to live with the intention of staying

equator imaginary line around the middle of a planet or body in space

lava tube natural tunnel formed by a lava flow

lunar having to do with a moon

module separate section that can be linked to other parts

orbit to travel around an object in space; an orbit is also the path an object follows while circling an object in space

probe small vehicle used to explore objects in outer space

propulsion thrust or power that makes an aeroplane or rocket move forward

radiation dangerous rays of energy given off by certain elements

satellite object that moves around a planet or other cosmic body; often a spacecraft used to send signals and information from one place to another

spacewalk period of time during which an astronaut leaves the spacecraft to move around in space

FIND OUT MORE

Neil Armstrong and Getting to the Moon (Adventures in Space), Ben Hubbard
(Raintree, 2016)

Neil Armstrong and the Moon Landings (Why Do We Remember?), Izzi Howell
(Franklin Watts, 2018)

The Moon (Astronaut Travel Guides), Chris Oxlade (Raintree, 2012)

To the Moon and Back: My Apollo 11 Adventure, National Geographic Kids with Buzz
Aldrin (National Geographic Kids, 2018)

WEBSITES

Build a moon habitat!
spaceplace.nasa.gov/Moon-habitat/en/

Facts about the moon
www.natgeokids.com/uk/discover/science/space/facts-about-the-moon/

Moon exploration
www.esa.int/esaKIDSen/SEMXR6WJD1E_OurUniverse_0.html

Moon mission
www.dkfindout.com/uk/space/moon-landings/

INDEX